THE LOST ORIGINAL

Kate Hendry

HAPPENSTANCE

ACKNOWLEDGMENTS:

Thanks are due to the editors of the following publications in
which some of these poems, or earlier versions, originally appeared:
Bare Fiction, The Compass Magazine, The Frogmore Papers, Gutter, The
Manchester Review, New Walk, The North, Northwords Now, Obsessed
with Pipework, Orbis, The Rialto, The Red Wheelbarrow, The Reader.

My love and thanks to Diana Hendry, Hamish Whyte, Vicki Feaver,
Elspeth Brown and Mario Relich for poetic advice and encouragement.

Printed by The Dolphin Press
www.dolphinpress.co.uk

Published in 2016 by HappenStance,
21 Hatton Green, Glenrothes, Fife KY7 4SD
nell@happenstancepress.com
www.happenstancepress.com

CONTENTS

for my family,
with love

Baked Beans

He'd already gone, when Mum told me—
to a room in the Alveston House Hotel.
Still a chance he'd come back home.

It was baked beans on toast, in the garden;
the green baize card table (brought out
for good weather) unfolded just for me.

After I'd been told, I ate up my food
and I took my empty plate, knife and fork
back inside and washed them up myself.

After the Divorce

All the leaving I had to do,
Bristol Parkway, Sheffield.
Weekends clamped by leaving.

Friday evenings—leaving her
by the waiting room, her winter coat
buttoned up for the dark drive home.

Sunday afternoons—leaving him
on the platform, mime-walking
away, his mouth gaping joke tears.

All my delayed trains—lost hours
between homes. Reading *Women in Love*.
Watching the night unfold.

Botanical Illustration

Published by Nuttall, Fisher and Dixon, Liverpool 1816

A leaving present to my parents
from Peggy Poole. On the back, in blue ink:
To keep in mind—Liverpool, botany, poetry.
With love to you both. Christmas 1970.

It was the year of my birth.
We'd moved south—my father to study plants,
my mother to write, away from *her* mother.
They hung the picture on the landing.

Thirty three years of divorce later
it's nailed behind my bathroom door—
the faded paper sitting squint,
the frame more black than gold.

It's an engraving of four leafy flowers,
stems growing through the airy soil
of small italic letters—Latin names
on one side, English on the other.

Annona, the paw paw, its fruit cut in two;
Ononis, early purple rest harrow;
Indigofera Anil, wild indigo;
Anemone japonica, windflower.

Yellow stamens, pale pink petals.
Just like those my father grew for my mother
in our north-facing garden,
the petals too thin to hang on through autumn.

The Art of Reading

In 1979 I read Enid Blyton
on the landing
in the yellow armchair.

My mother at the end of the corridor,
my brother upstairs, my father
renovating his latest rusty mangle.

Into the yellow leather armchair,
first thing in the morning.
I read non-stop.

My mother, at the far end
of the corridor, with laundry basket
and damp sheets.

My brother, in his red room,
practising hitches and turns
from the *Ashley Book of Knots*.

My father, in the garage,
oiling wooden rollers,
building up layers of turquoise paint.

I read *The Magic Faraway Tree*
and finished it in one day,
starting the next one straight away.

I read till the sheets
were folded and the paint
was dry and the knots were all undone.

My father thought it dross.
He took his Acme mangle
with him when he left.

Before A and B

Reading Doctor Faustus, going from the A text to the B text
and back again, working out what's in one but not the other,
(the funny bits, an extra pope, Faustus's dismemberment),

I think of my parents' houses, my A and B homes,
how they each have furniture (the green velvet armchair,
the piano) from the first home, the ur-home.

Long gone, it rattles me, much as Marlowe's urtext
haunts critics, makes them believe in a forgotten storeroom
in a London lodging house, where a leather trunk holds

that script, the lost original, and the letter which explains
who wanted him dead. Finding Dr Faustus would be like
me going back to when there was only one home

and the record collection hadn't been divided and the cellar
was stacked with too many bottles of undrinkable 1976
home-made wine because there was a glut of parsnips that year.

It wouldn't be like Walter Greg's attempt after the war
to rebuild Doctor Faustus, taking the best bits from A and B,
leaving out the gratuitous jokes, trying to make something

beautiful and dramatic. One man's fantasy—no one reads it now.
And it wouldn't be like Greg's parallel text, with A and B
sitting opposite each other, A holding its tongue while B starts

on a new point, leaving the reader waiting (for one to begin,
for the other to stop) and struggling to match up lines
that never, after the opening scene, quite agree

and even when the characters are doing the same thing
on both pages their words are different, like they're yelling
at each other and you can no longer hear either of them

let alone yourself, and you almost feel grateful for the gaps,
the blanks, page after page of emptiness.

Heart Failure

Another conversation with my father about death:
'You can stab your heart—you won't feel it,
the heart's autonomous,' he says. I twist
my daughter's abandoned pipe cleaner

into a blue, three-petalled flower.
My father's heart is doing its own thing—
racing blood around his body too fast, forcing
him to lie down. Only he won't.

OK, maybe he'll give up climbing mountains.
And caffeine. He's agreed to get someone in
to climb on the roof when slates have slipped.
But slowing down? Stopping?

***

He tells me he felt it coming on one day
last week, driving home from the city:
his heart's in his throat, he can't catch
his breath. What should he do? Lie down?

Only sixty-three miles—it takes him an hour
and five minutes on a good day. That day
he had to keep a steady speed. No point
pulling over to a lay-by. He could drive through it.

***

I imagine him clipping the edge of the road,
crashing down a heathered slope, trying to keep
his hands on the wheel, his foot on the brake
his lungs dragging in air. *Breathe, breathe,*

he's telling himself. Why can't he do something
to stop the car gliding over cotton grass,
sphagnum moss? An alluvial river?
He's noted the water's snaking path before—

always meant to stop the car, get out, examine
eroded banks. The words come at him—
meander, oxbow. The geography of it
first hand. The water rising up the windscreen.

***

On the sofa, he tells me how the cardiologist
will burn his heart with radio waves.
He wants it done before the doctors say
he's too old for surgery. He wants his life back.

The next day, he heads home. He texts me:
*There's fresh snow on the hills. It's lambing
season. In the front lawn the first
bluebell shoots are coming through.*

First Term, Glasgow 1989

By the Royal Bank of Scotland on Byres Road
you told me. 'I've done the test,' you said.
'I'm pregnant.' You were a year older than me.
You rolled the joints and played me your music.
You knew what to do about men and sex.

At the hospital they wouldn't let you out
unless someone came to pick you up.
I kept a black taxi waiting, while I waited for you.
The nurses pushed open swing doors, letting them slap
shut on green beds and you, sitting on the edge.

The taxi took us to Queen Margaret Halls
where I saw you to your room like a first date.
Awkward goodbyes at the door before setting off
to the theatre. An immediate betrayal.
It was Macbeth at The Citizens, my ticket pre-booked

because my first essay was due at 5 p.m., December 6th.
Consider the importance (or otherwise)
of the witches in a new production of the play.
No extensions would be given, except for
certified medical reasons. I had to go, I had

to leave you, even though you were still
crying, even though you hadn't stopped
crying since I picked you up from Stobhill
in the black cab, the same cab, its engine running
outside, which waited to take me away.

Catching Up with My Little Brother

—for Fergus

I was nineteen when you were born.
Waiting for you shortened that first scary
winter term away from home.
I saw you only hours old, little brother,
two weeks late; wrinkled skin, big feet.

Now it's me that's running late. I catch up
with you at six, but find you've just turned eight.
I've tracked your growing up, but not come close
to making out your boy things, your reserve.
Just the other day you caught me watching.
'What?' you growled. And to my questions
answered 'stuff', 'dunno' and ''s alright'.
I sneaked around your room in school time
compiled a list, to find you in the way your 'stuff'
fits together. But I'm no nearer.

I nose through memories, make another list:
At two you pulled off all my castor-oil plant's leaves.
At five I taught you *Three Blind Mice* on lettered piano keys.
(Now one finger drums the tune to *Mission Impossible*).
I've brushed your teeth, had baths with you. Read you stories.
Pushed you in your pram, on the swing, on your bike.
Carried you on my shoulders, on my back, in my arms.
I've written four poems about you
and known you for ten years.

When I visit, you say (but not to me) you want me to stay.
Goodbye is standing on each other's feet.

My Father Carries His Death to Me

'I thought I was dying,' he says, 'dying.
I said to J on the night of the party,
I'm not going to make it till the end.'

I turn from the washing up
to hear him. He's making coffee
on the other side of the kitchen.

Adrienne Rich carried her death
in her pocket like a raincoat.
Mine is with me at the table

like the shells I've brought in,
wet and glowing from the beach,
though their colours fade inside.

His death is with him like the small
white stones he lines up by his front door
to help him find his way home in the dark.

Valentine

A large red sun sets as I drive home.
You're at work.
I plant cardboard cut-out hearts
where you'll find them at midnight

in the teabag box,
in the biscuit tin,
by your toothbrush.

I keep the stove going.
I sit your slippers by the hearth.
Is that it?
Remembering to leave a little love
where it can be seen?

Permission

I'm running late for work. The baby needs
a nappy change. In the still-dark morning
I lay her on the bed. You sit up,
as if it's your birthday and you've been waiting
for this one present, which I place on your lap.

You and our daughter. I watch you loving her
like you're allowed. For this short time
of her babyhood you can baste her with love.
No talking to work out, no fighting over food
or bed-times. She lies there for you

as you dangle your fingers over her tummy
and kiss her feet. 'You're in love with her,'
I say. 'Who?' you say—it's your game.
I'm not to catch you loving her. It's done
in private, in dark rooms, when I'm rushing out.

Your Voice

I collect your words—
first *shoes* then *cot* and *book*.
You say *baby* to the mirror
and at fifteen months, *key* and *kiss*.

Then one day you want me
and I've gone out. I comfort you
on the phone and hear,
as if for the first time, your voice,

gruff and grown up, and that word,
learnt months ago, the one
I forgot to date or record
until now—*Mummy, Mummy.*

Skin

He was born in winter so I wrapped him up:
shawl, mittens, hat. One year on, I rarely see
his neck, buried under folds of chin,
moist and secret, like unpeeled fruit.

One year on, I don't know his bones.
His hands have no knuckles.
His knees are solid tubes of fat.
His feet are thick like steaks.

Each night, I strip off layers of clothes.
Naked on the bed, my body brackets his.
He wakes, turns to me. Fingers grip
my lips, my nose, my skin.

Discussing My Death

Tea time—sausages, peas and chips.
We're discussing what happens when you fall,
counting up the ambulances we've been in.
One when I burnt my hand, one when I fell downstairs.

'Did you die?' you ask. Oh, to not know.
To talk about death as if it's a game.
To gun people dead and bring them back to life.
To kill me off when I've been mean.

Sometimes you cry 'I'll miss you when you're dead,'
no notion of your grown-up, stronger self
or that you might not even like me much by then.
'I'll keep your bones,' you say, 'that's what's left of you.'

You decide you'll make them into weapons
like the arrowheads that cave-men made.
You ask if it would be against the law.
I say 'you can't keep bones' and repeat my line

(stolen from Larkin) that what remains of us is love.
You're onto pudding—ask for more ice cream.
I think of my keepsakes—baby shoes, hats, teeth—
a store to ward off all the loss to come.

Dream Fight

I dream of you, spending all our money.
You've done a bunk, gone to Bangkok to shop.
I'm angry, fly there to fight.

You drive me into suburbs where streets end
in jungle, to buy a coat you want.
You spend. I yell. We've been at it for days.

In time, I forget to keep it up.
We can't help talking like friends.
The daily tasks spawn conversation.
Our row sinks into the hot earth like hour-old rain.

I wake to find my head is full of you.
We've spent days together in my sleep.
The dream-you soaks up space between us—
All that talking we did. All my unquenched rage.

Identifying Flowers

My father knew the Latin names,
family, subfamily, genus, species.
He told me them, over and over
on weekend walks down the Pithay.

By eleven, old enough to learn myself,
he bought me my own copy
of Keble Martin's *Concise British Flora*
for my birthday.

He'd left home by then,
had moved to a basement flat,
1, All Saints Road, Bristol
and our weekends were museums

but he marked the book and graded
the families: 'Very Very Important,'
'Important' and 'Not'. I was to master
Compositae, Rosaceae, Gramineae.

I took the long way home from school
to pick flowers. At home I'd lay them
next to Keble Martin's pictures
to find their family and name.

Plate 47: ragwort, groundsel.
Then I'd press them between the pages
till their stems hardened
and their yellow petals turned brown.

An Appointment at the National Library of Scotland

What can I show my father, when he comes to stay
with me? Edinburgh—a city he frowns on
for its wealth and power and childhood memories
of Sunday visits to Great Aunt Enid in her villa
near the zoo, the hard chair at the hot bay window

where (*Sit still, keep quiet, wait for mother*)
he picked orange peel from fruitcake.
What can I show him, once the tour is over
of my too small flat, my windowless kitchen?
The view to the Botanics from our dining table?

We'll have no time to sightsee—Thursday morning
before his 12.45 train home. So I offer him
a visit to the Library, as if it's mine.
I know he's tried before; was told off at the door
for turning up without warning or proper ID.

I know which forms he needs, where the lockers are.
I'll bring a pound coin for his coat and bag,
lend him a pencil, take him to the lift
up to the special collections reading room,
to see notebook drafts of Sorley MacLean's poems.

We'll try to decipher the Gaelic, find 'Hallaig',
(long blu-tacked to my father's bathroom wall).
He'll whisper the first line to me—
'*Tha tìm, am fiadh, an coille Hallaig*'—
while I stare through crossings out to the words beneath.

What the Fridge Wants

It stays awake all night
grumbling to itself in the dark.

Every hour it drums at the wall as if
it wants to come in,

needs company. Food.
I shudder out of sleep.

I want to rip out its innards.
Toxic fuel will seep between the tiles.

Morning. I size up its fat, white bulk.
My narrow kitchen.

There's nowhere else for it to fit.
When I open it, it goes quiet.

I squint against its bright inner light.
Behind the leftovers—ripe brie, sour wine—

there's breakfast.
              Milk, butter, jam. Let
its clamorous door swing back.

On Coming to Love the Dog after Twenty Months

Every night she goes out into the woods.
We hear her barking—at deer, the fox,
pheasants—whatever we can't see.
But this night she's gone silent
and by bed-time she's still not home.

I call and call. 'Bramble, what's this?'
It's our understanding—
'this'—a biscuit—in my hand.
I have to go to bed.
You go out with the torch.

Later, when you come to bed,
I don't ask. What do I care?
Stupid hound, always running off.
She casts long black hair on every floor.
Lies, wet, on my wool rug. Smells.

But I wake at half past three, listening.
Not for our daughter's cries
or our son's winter cough,
but for Bramble's bark.
I think about life without her,
hair-free, clean, fragrant.

I go downstairs, click open the door,
flick the light and there she is,
instantly awake and overjoyed,
thumping her tail, bowing her head,
skitting across the skiddy kitchen floor.

Like when I come home,
and the table's laid for tea,
the curtains are drawn, the fire's lit
and she's the first to greet me.

Counting

We're in Costa on high stools
by the window, watching buses go by.
You ask me if I'll help you
count to one hundred. We're to take turns.
You start at twenty one.

At forty five we break to laugh.
At sixty four you pause for a sip
of hot chocolate and to squeeze
the two pink marshmallows
you're keeping till last.

Our counting starts again.
I try a stumble at seventy six
by repeating your number
but you catch me out
and put your sticky fingers on my lips.

At ninety, I want to stave off ending;
I slow down, mumble,
feign confusion. Ninety what?
But you urge me on.
It's me who has to say *one hundred*.

You bite the first marshmallow.
'You had all the evens,' you explain
as if I should have known
it was always my task
to be in charge of endings.